DATE DUE			

HARRY TRUMAN

President Truman in the photograph of himself that he liked best. *Harry S. Truman Library*

HARRY TRUMAN

by DORIS FABER

Illustrated with photographs

Abelard-Schuman

NEW YORK   LONDON

© Copyright 1972 by Doris Faber
Library of Congress Catalogue Card Number: 72-2076
ISBN: 0 200 71905 X Trade
ISBN: 0 200 71906 8 GB

NEW YORK
Abelard-Schuman
Limited
257 Park Ave. S.
10010

LONDON
Abelard-Schuman
Limited
158 Buckingham Palace Road SW1
and
24 Market Square, Aylesbury

An INTEXT Publisher
Published on the same day in Canada
by Longman Canada Limited.

Printed in the United States of America

Library of Congress Cataloging in Publication Data
Faber, Doris, 1924–
   Harry Truman.

   SUMMARY: A biography of the farm boy from Missouri who
became a Senator, Vice-President, and finally President of the United
States.
   Bibliography: p.
   1. Truman, Harry S., Pres. U. S., 1884–
Juvenile literature. [1. Truman, Harry S., Pres.
U. S. 1884–   2. Presidents]
E814.F3   973.918′092′4 [B] [92]   72–2076
ISBN 0–200–71905–X
ISBN 0–200–71906–8 (lib bdg.)

Contents

CONTENTS

List of Illustrations

1

Fireworks

A frog jumped up out of the high grass. The little boy jumped too. Whoosh! The frog leaped again. The boy followed right along, slapping his knees with delight. He laughed so loudly that his grandmother stopped gathering berries.

"Well," she said, "I've never yet seen a young one with such a sense of humor."

Harry Truman was just two years old then. He found out later that his family was living on a small farm near the western border of Missouri.

He had been born farther south in the same state, on May 8, 1884. His birthplace was Lamar, a sleepy village where his father had tried to start

The house where Harry Truman was born on May 8, 1884, in Lamar, Missouri. *Harry S. Truman Library*

a mule-trading business. John Truman did not succeed in this venture, however, nor in the others that followed it, so Harry's family kept moving from town to town during his early years.

Sometimes they returned to the large house where his mother had grown up. Born Martha Ellen Young, she was the daughter of a prosperous farmer. Harry and Grandpa Young became great friends during these long visits. When Harry was only five, Grandpa Young took him to the county fair six days in a row!

Even if he wasn't always lucky enough to have an unlimited supply of striped candy and peanuts the way he did at the fair, Harry still found something special about every single day. On Grandpa Young's farm, he made a pet of a particular pig. He went climbing in the hayloft with his younger brother, Vivian. He fed and brushed the Shetland pony Grandpa Young bought for him.

Harry had an especially good time on Sundays, when a crowd of aunts, uncles, and cousins came to dinner. The Trumans and the Youngs had known each other back in the old days before both families left Kentucky to settle in Missouri. They told exciting stories about their trip westward by wagon train and about the Civil War. Harry spent hour after hour listening to these tales. That was how he first got interested in American history.

When Harry was six, his father started a new livestock-trading business in the town of Independence, which was just twenty miles from the cattle markets of Kansas City. This new business went well.

Harry liked living in Independence. He could still visit Grandpa Young every Sunday, for their new home was just a comfortable buggy ride from the farm. And he still had plenty of pets because there were ponies, goats and mules out back in the big fenced-in yard where his father conducted his business.

Besides, Harry's mother took him to Sunday school soon after they moved, and he was assigned the seat right in back of a girl with the prettiest yellow curls he had ever seen. Her name was Elizabeth Virginia Wallace, but everybody called her Bess. Harry thought she must be the most beautiful girl in the whole world.

Partly because he was so eager to see Bess more often—and maybe even talk to her, if he ever felt brave enough—Harry begged his mother to let

him enter the first grade that fall. But he had another reason, too, for wanting to start school. He
was eager to learn to read.

He could already puzzle out the letters in the
family Bible, but these were much larger than
the letters in the other books his mother had on the
parlor shelf. It bothered him that he couldn't make
any sense out of these other books, even when his
mother tried to help him.

"Once I get to school, I'll catch on," he told her.
"I'm sure I will!"

Yet his mother did not agree about school.
"You'll have to wait, Harry," she said.

He had to wait two full years while Mrs. Truman kept worrying about him. Though she believed that Harry was brighter than the average
boy, because of the way he enjoyed listening to
grown-up talk, she was afraid that his reading
difficulty would prevent him from becoming a
good student.

"What's the use of sending him to school?" she
asked her husband. "He would only be laughed
at, and I won't stand for that!"

So Harry had to be content helping his father
and playing with Vivian and their baby sister,

Mary Jane—till at last his mother discovered what his trouble was.

On the Fourth of July when Harry was eight years old, a glorious display of fireworks lit the sky over Independence. Harry clapped excitedly each time a crackling bang sounded, but his mother noticed a strange fact. He never seemed to look up at the exploding red and green and purple stars. Suddenly she understood!

Mrs. Truman tugged at her husband's arm.

"Harry can't see!" she said.

"What's that?" John Truman demanded.

"He just can't see anything too small or too far away."

She was right. The next day, she hitched up the buggy and drove Harry to Kansas City. When they returned, he was wearing the thickest pair of eyeglasses ever seen in Independence.

2

"Old Four Eyes"

Fortunately, Harry never minded being teased. He would just grin when other boys shouted, "Here comes Old Four Eyes!" Yet those thick eyeglasses that he had to wear definitely set him apart.

"Leave 'em off and come fishing with me," his brother begged him one sunny Saturday.

"I can't, Viv," Harry said. "I've gotten used to them, and I feel blind as a mole without them."

"Then keep 'em on and come fishing anyway!" Vivian urged.

Harry shook his head. "You know what Mama would say if all that amount of glass got broken.

But don't you fret about me—I really do think fishing is pretty boring."

Playing ball was another matter. Harry wished he could take part in the lively games in the empty lot down the street. Still he saw no point worrying over something that couldn't be helped. He would rather look on the bright side and now he could go to school. There he learned to read every size of type practically overnight.

"Why, you're turning into a regular bookworm, Harry!" his mother told him delightedly.

Afternoons when school was out, he'd sprawl on his stomach on the kitchen floor with his nose in a book. He read all the books on his mother's shelf and he read almost every book in the Independence Public Library, even the encyclopedias.

With all this extra reading, Harry was able to skip a grade. Then he was only one grade behind Bess Wallace whose yellow curls and blue eyes still struck him as the most beautiful sight he'd ever seen. Yet every time he did see Bess on the playground, or in Sunday school, Harry's tongue played tricks on him. He still couldn't manage to say one single word to her.

Usually, Harry had no trouble talking and joking. Even if he couldn't play ball, he did figure out how to join the fun when a boy gave him the hint he needed.

"Four Eyes, you look just like a wise old owl," this boy said.

"Good!" Harry shot right back. "Then I can be the umpire." From that day on, he got a lot of practice in settling disputes.

As Harry grew bigger, his father gave him more jobs to do, such as driving the family's cow out to pasture every morning and bringing her back to the barn toward evening.

When he was ten, he and his brother both caught diphtheria, but Vivian got better quickly. Harry wasn't so lucky. For six months, he couldn't move his legs and he had to be wheeled around the house in a baby buggy.

"Suppose you can't *ever* walk again," Vivian said one day.

"I will, and that's all there is to it!" Harry answered.

As soon as he did feel well, he worked so hard on his studies that he more than made up for lost time. Instead of going into the fourth grade the following fall, he was promoted right into the fifth grade. At last, he was in the same class with Bess Wallace and the other boys and girls his own age.

Finally, Harry even talked to Bess. "I'll carry your books home," he told her one afternoon.

From then on, through the rest of grade school and high school, too, Harry carried Bess's books almost every afternoon. Sometimes they studied Latin together, or went skating when the pond was frozen. Everybody in town knew that Harry Truman was sweet on Bess Wallace, but nobody teased Harry about this more than Bess herself.

"I declare, you're hopeless, Harry," she told him one afternoon when they were fifteen. Her blue eyes sparkled with fun as she added, "If you won't learn to dance this very week, I believe I'll carry my own books."

"Now don't you do that, Bess," he answered. "I'm going to learn, when I get around to it."

But Harry felt clumsy as an ox whenever he tried to dance. Besides, he thought he had better things to do with his time, though he wouldn't say so to Bess. He liked playing the piano much more than he liked dancing, so he practiced his piano-playing several hours every day. He also had a job

Harry Truman at the age of thirteen. *Harry S. Truman Library*

sweeping out the local drugstore every morning before school. He enjoyed going to political meetings with his father, who had become interested in politics. Of course, he also had schoolwork to do.

Harry was hoping that he would be able to go to college. Not many boys or girls from small towns like Independence went on to college in those days, but since Harry was one of the best students in his class his mother thought he ought to, and he agreed with her.

So did Harry's father, till a sudden spell of bad luck hit his business. During Harry's last year of high school, John Truman lost all his money. Instead of going to college after he graduated, Harry had to go to work.

3

To Work

Harry tried all sorts of jobs during the next several years. He worked for the railroad, in a newspaper office and then for a bank.

While his father kept hoping to make a new start, Harry and Vivian both earned as much money as they could. Although these years were hard because the family had to give up their comfortable home in Independence and move to a tiny house in Kansas City, Harry made many new friends.

Now that he was old enough not to worry about breaking his eyeglasses, he even joined a group of men who spent their spare time training to be soldiers. If a war ever came, he wanted to be able to do his share toward defending his country.

As far as other people could tell, young Harry Truman was perfectly content with the way his life was turning out. Yet he still felt disappointed about not going to college. His interest in American history was stronger than ever and he had a secret dream. He wanted to be a United States senator someday. Unless he got a college education, he thought the chances for seeing his dream come true were extremely slim. Yet he never complained.

"There's no sense crying over spilled milk," he cheerfully reminded his sister Mary Jane. Because they both loved piano music, and often played duets together, these two had become special friends. She was the only one he ever told about his dream of being a senator.

Mary Jane thought her big brother should aim even higher. "You ought to be president of the United States!" she said.

That made Harry grin at her. "Will you visit me in the White House?" he asked.

When Harry was twenty, the Trumans had a visitor at their own little house in Kansas City.

Farmer Truman (second from left) posing on a hay wagon with some friends and relatives. *Kansas City* Star, *courtesy of Harry S. Truman Library*

Uncle Harrison Young came and urged them to move back onto Grandpa Young's farm. This seemed a good plan for several reasons.

Although Grandpa Young himself had died a few years ago, Grandma Young still lived there and was trying to keep the place going with hired help. Wouldn't it be much better, Uncle Harrison asked, if John Truman and his sons took over the running of the farm for her?

Everybody except Harry liked this idea. He felt that by leaving the city, where sooner or later he might save enough money to go to college, he was giving up any real hope for playing some part in the government of his country. Yet he never said a word, even to Mary Jane, about his feelings on this subject. To him, his family was more important than any dream of his own.

So Harry Truman put on overalls and spent the next thirteen years as a plain dirt farmer. He plowed and planted, he pitched hay and milked cows. He kept doing the chores that had to be done while the seasons came and went.

In a few years, Grandma Young died and the farm now belonged to Harry's mother. Harry's brother married and moved to a farm of his own. Then Harry's father, who had not really been strong enough for heavy work, became sick and died. That left Harry all alone to take care of his mother and sister, and to manage a large farm.

If he had been free to do just as he pleased, Harry would have liked more than ever to be living elsewhere. In 1914, the year before his father died, a great war had broken out in Europe. Any newspaper reader knew that England and France were fighting against Germany, and that many other nations on the other side of the world were also involved in the conflict.

Why had such a fierce struggle erupted? With his deep interest in history, Harry longed to learn more about the basic causes of the war. He wanted to test some of his own views, too. In his opinion, the United States had become so powerful that sooner or later it would surely be drawn into the fighting. Did serious students of history agree with him?

Although he was already beyond the usual age for enrolling in college, he would have jumped at the opportunity to do more studying. Then he might still stand some chance of having an influence on the course his country took during the years to come.

But as things were, all he could do was to study by himself. He went through every book about world affairs he could find in the library. No matter how tired he was after he finished his farm chores, he did not let himself neglect his reading.

Neither did he neglect his farming. Since he seemed fated to spend his life working on the land, he thought he might just as well do the best possible job of it. So he kept trying new kinds of seeds and asking advice from experts. As a result, he made his farm one of the finest in the area. Usually, one evening a week, he put on city clothes and drove his new little automobile into Kansas City to meet his friends who were training to be soldiers. On Sundays, he drove over to Independence and called on Bess Wallace.

For he had never stopped thinking she was the prettiest girl in the world and he still hoped she would marry him. Yet he was just an ordinary farmer, while her family lived in a fine house. If only he could do something to prove that he was worthy of her!

At the age of thirty-three, he was still wondering how he could ask Bess to become a farmer's wife. Then in 1917, the United States entered the terrible war that had been raging in Europe for three years—and Harry Truman became a soldier.

4

The Dizzy D

Men with even a small amount of military training were badly needed by the army in 1917, so Harry Truman had no trouble getting accepted for active duty. Eyeglasses and all, he was made a lieutenant.

While his sister bravely set about trying to run the farm all by herself, Lieutenant Truman spent several months learning how big guns worked. As an officer in the branch of the army called the field artillery, he would have to give orders for the aiming and firing of these heavy cannon.

But before being put in charge of his own com-

First Lieutenant Harry S. Truman *Harry S. Truman Library*

pany of soldiers, he got a different sort of job. At an army camp in Oklahoma, he had to open a new store where men receiving their basic training could buy such items as writing paper and candy. Although he had never had the slightest experience in storekeeping, he learned that, too. By the time he was transferred, he had made a profit of $15,000 for the army!

Then he had to pass a much harder test. In a mass of men wearing khaki-colored uniforms, he marched onto a train bound for New York City. There he boarded a ship which steamed across the ocean toward the fighting front in France. When he landed, Lieutenant Truman was put in command of Battery D in a field artillery unit.

Battery D had already made quite a name for itself. Many of its men came from rough neighborhoods in Kansas City, and they were a rowdy group who didn't like taking orders. While going through their advanced training to prepare them for battle, they had played so many tricks on their previous commander that they had become known as "The Dizzy D."

Lieutenant Truman liked a joke as much as any man, but he did not think this bloody war was any laughing matter. So he called Battery D together the day he took command, and said crisply:

"I didn't come over here to get along with you. You've got to get along with me. If there are any of you who can't, speak up right now!"

There was a mean glint in Lieutenant Truman's eyes behind his glasses. Nobody in Battery D spoke up. From then on, they and their new commander got along without further trouble.

In fact, a rare closeness grew up between the men of The Dizzy D and their commanding officer. He could be mean when he had to, but soon it became perfectly plain that he would much rather be friendly. During off hours, he even took a hand in many a card game—and he didn't mind a bit when he lost.

After Battery D moved up to the front line, Lieutenant Truman was promoted to the rank of captain. But none of his own men called him Captain Truman. To them, he was always "Captain Harry."

Week after week, they lived together in muddy ditches. All day and all night, the boom of their big guns and of enemy cannon hurt their ears. They were in danger every minute. Yet Harry

31

Truman would always look back on these months as one of the high points of his life.

For he discovered then that he could lead other men, and they would follow him willingly. He found out that he was fearless under fire. When the war ended on November 11, 1918, and he could start thinking about his own personal concerns again, he had a new self-confidence.

As soon as Captain Harry Truman got back to Missouri, he asked Bess Wallace to be his wife, and they were married just one month later in Independence.

5

Captain Harry's Ups and Downs

After a honeymoon trip to Chicago, Mr. and Mrs. Harry Truman settled down in the Wallace family's large white house in Independence. Nobody thought that the new Mrs. Truman ought to be a farmer's wife. The Truman land was rented out, with Harry's mother and sister keeping the farmhouse for their own use, but one big question remained.

How was a man of thirty-five, who had very little experience in any line of work except farming, going to support a wife now?

As Captain Harry, he had made countless friends and with the coming of peace, they did not forget him. As soon as he decided what he wanted to do, he had no trouble finding old army buddies willing to help him.

His first idea was to open a men's clothing store. Back in Oklahoma, a soldier named Eddie Jacobson had worked with him in the army store. So in 1919 a sign, announcing that Truman & Jacobson were going into business, appeared on a window opposite the leading hotel in Kansas City.

For two years, the new store was a great success. Former soldiers often stopped in to talk over old times with Captain Harry, or to ask his advice about some problem of their own. While they were there, they bought a few shirts or ties.

Gradually money got scarcer when hard times began to affect business all over the country. Captain Harry still had plenty of old friends to keep him company, but they no longer bought any new clothes.

"We'll have to quit, Harry," Eddie Jacobson said one evening.

"I can see that," his partner agreed, "but I don't want anybody else to suffer for our bad luck."

So he paid back every penny he had borrowed for fixing up the store, although it took him several years to do it. It was during this time that he finally got started in politics.

He got his chance because one of his friends knew "Boss" Tom Pendergast, a powerful man in Missouri's Democratic party. This friend passed along the word that Captain Harry was a good Democrat who would make a popular candidate out in Jackson County where Independence was located.

"Boss" Pendergast put Truman on the party ticket to run for the post of county commissioner. But it was Truman himself who convinced people to vote for him.

He loaded two bags of cement in the back of his small car so that it wouldn't bounce too hard on bumpy roads. Then he drove to every farm in the county, and he promised every farmer that if he were elected he would make sure the roads were repaired. He won the election by a surprisingly large vote.

And he did get the roads fixed. Even so, because of a fight within the Democratic party, he was defeated when he ran for a second term two years later.

That was in 1924, the year his wife presented

him with a baby daughter they named Mary Margaret. To meet his responsibilities toward his family, the new father found a job in a Kansas City office. But Harry Truman had no intention of quitting politics.

When the next county election rolled around, his name was on the ballot again, this time at the top of the list. And this time he got all the votes he needed to win.

Then he became the head of the board of county commissioners. Although his job still had more to do with fixing roads and keeping county buildings in good condition than with court cases, he was entitled to be called Judge Truman.

Among the residents of Jackson County in Missouri, Judge Truman made more and more friends. He did this in a variety of ways. Being the sort of man who sincerely enjoyed meeting other people, he was never too busy to "visit with" anybody stopping by his office. Besides attending regular meetings of his old army buddies, he also joined several businessmen's clubs. Whenever someone was needed to help out in a worthy cause, Judge Truman stepped forward.

Most important of all, he took his official duties

seriously. During the late 1920s, while the nation was going through a period of unmatched prosperity, Judge Truman saw to it that Jackson County got many long overdue public improvements. New roads were constructed, two new court houses were built, and so was a new hospital.

Even after the good times suddenly ended in 1929, Judge Truman kept pushing these and other projects toward completion. Widespread hardship was caused by the collapse of the country's main stock market in New York City. When prices tumbled at this trading center, thousands of factories from coast to coast were forced to close. Millions of workers lost their jobs. Fear and confusion spread everywhere. But Judge Truman stayed calm.

The United States had weathered plenty of storms already, he said, and it would survive this one, too.

His hopeful outlook made him a strong supporter of the new president who was elected in 1932. Franklin D. Roosevelt told his fellow citizens, "The only thing we have to fear is fear itself." Judge Truman fully agreed. To put the nation back on the right track, President Roosevelt proposed a program he called the "New Deal." Judge Truman, who still had a special interest in American history, spent many thoughtful hours studying newspaper accounts about New Deal measures.

Social Security for the aged, emergency aid for the unemployed, new help for the nation's farmers —all of these were part of President Roosevelt's program. They aroused heated debate. Some people insisted that the federal government in Washington had no right to pass any laws about such matters. But Judge Truman decided this viewpoint was wrong and he felt particularly cheerful whenever a New Deal measure was adopted.

Yet his day-to-day concerns were still limited by the boundaries of Jackson County. Every two years he ran for a new term, and he devoted his energy to local problems. Even his political opponents admitted that he was an honest man with an unusual talent for taking care of public business, but nobody expected him to seek any higher office. Judge Truman himself almost forgot about his dream of someday being Senator Truman.

6

Luck and Pluck

On May 8, 1934, Judge Truman quietly celebrated his fiftieth birthday. One week later he received a telephone call. He was told that "Boss"
Tom Pendergast's most trusted assistant wanted
to see him.

On his way into the city, Truman thought over
some possible reasons for this summons. Was there
a problem in Jackson County that he didn't know
about? Would he be asked to do something he
didn't think was right?

During all his years in office, he had been left
pretty much on his own by the Pendergast machine—and that suited him fine. He couldn't help

but be aware that the machine had a bad reputa-
tion. Tom Pendergast himself was supposed to be
too friendly with criminals. Yet Harry Truman
couldn't forget that Pendergast had given him his
first chance to run in an election. Now if Tom
wanted a favor in return, it would be hard to re-
fuse.

What Tom Pendergast did want stunned Truman.

"The Boss asked me to sound you out," Pendergast's assistant said. "Would you be interested in
running for a bigger job this fall?" The man
paused, and puffed on a big cigar. "Running for
senator," he said through a haze of smoke.

Truman could hardly believe he had heard right.

"You did say senator?" he asked. But already his
mind was considering every side of this astonish-
ing offer. From time to time, he had let it be known
that he would like to run for some other office
higher than the one he held, and always he had
been ignored. Now suddenly he was being given
a much greater opportunity than he had dared to
suggest. Why?

In a minute, he thought of the answer. Because
the Pendergast machine had been getting blasted

Harry Truman speaking from the courthouse steps in Independence, Missouri, during his campaign for the U.S. Senate in 1934. *Harry S. Truman Library*

in the newspapers lately, Tom was having trouble finding a candidate willing to run. Yet if Tom Pendergast imagined that Harry Truman was just a puppet who would take orders from him, he was mistaken!

"I'd like twenty-four hours to think about this," Truman said solemnly.

That night he had a long talk with his wife. As far as he was concerned, Bess Truman was "the boss." She had no ambition to live anywhere else in the world except Independence, but she would not let her husband give up his dream for her sake.

"You'd be sorry the rest of your days if you didn't take this chance," she said. "So go ahead. If the best man does win, I guess I'll get used to Washington."

First she had to get used to seeing her husband insulted in print. "Who is Judge Truman?" newspapers all over Missouri asked sarcastically. "Truman is a nobody," one editor wrote. "He's just an errand boy for Tom Pendergast," another writer insisted.

But Truman himself was too busy to pay much attention to the newspapers. For he found that he had a real fight on his hands. Two prominent Democrats who hated Pendergast decided to challenge the machine by seeking their party's nomination for senator on their own. That meant there had to be a special primary election in August to settle the question of who would be the Democratic candidate in November. Because these other men were much more widely known throughout the state than Harry Truman was, it appeared that Truman was doomed to lose to one or the other.

Almost everybody except Harry Truman thought so. He just got into his small car and spent week after week driving along Missouri's back roads. He stopped in post offices and at church picnics. He talked to farmers and to former soldiers. Although he made a poor job of it when he tried to make speeches at big meetings, he did much better before small groups.

Then his simple words hit home. People believed him when he promised that he would speak up for the average citizen if they sent him to Washington. Plain folks liked him because he looked like one of them. Almost every time he shook a stranger's hand, Harry Truman reminded that stranger of someone in his own family.

When the primary election took place, Truman was back with his wife feeling tired, yet satisfied. He had done his best, and he thought it would be good enough. It was. He won that primary, surprising all the experts.

After that he had hardly any trouble beating his Republican opponent in November. Harry Truman had taken advantage of a piece of luck, and by his own efforts made the most of it. Six months after his fiftieth birthday, he left Missouri for Washington, D.C.

7

Freshman...

Mrs. Harry Truman and ten-year-old Mary Margaret took their seats in the visitors' gallery. Down below them on the floor of the United States Senate, white-haired Vice-President Garner gave a signal. Thirteen men stepped forward. The solemn ceremony of swearing in new members was about to begin.

Standing with the other "freshmen" senators, Harry Truman of Missouri was not ashamed of the mist that clouded his eyeglasses. Here he was, after a plain country boyhood and not even a college education, preparing to join one of the most respected law-making bodies the world had ever known. He breathed a silent prayer that he would prove worthy of the trust that had been placed in him.

Then Truman's mood suddenly changed. He could never stay serious for too long. He looked straight up at Mary Margaret in the visitors' section—and he winked at her.

It was fortunate that Senator Truman had this gift of being able to keep from feeling puffed up with a sense of his own importance. For during his first months in Washington, he learned that although he was a big hero to his mother back in Missouri, here in the nation's capital he didn't rate very high.

With no other income except his salary, he could not afford to live in grand style. Instead he rented a small apartment just off Connecticut Avenue, and Mrs. Truman did the cooking because they could not spare money for a maid. To save the expense of hiring a secretary, she also typed letters for him while Mary Margaret was in school.

In the Senate itself, the new senator from Missouri was merely one of thirteen newcomers serving their first term. All of these freshmen were supposed to listen and learn for a few years before they started making speeches or sponsoring laws. Nobody paid too much attention to any of them, but Senator Truman got even less attention than his fellow freshmen.

This was because "Boss" Tom Pendergast had backed Harry Truman in his fight to win election. As one of the last of the old-time political bosses, Pendergast had come to be widely criticized. Other political figures were eager to make it clear that they disapproved of Pendergast. So they treated Pendergast's candidate coldly.

Senator Truman felt sure that sooner or later he would be able to show Washington he was his own man, not just a Pendergast follower. But he did not help his case by his folksy way of talking to newspaper reporters.

"I'm just a farmer boy from Jackson County," he told them. Then even fair-minded writers poked fun at him in print for bragging about how unfit he was to be a senator.

Gradually, though, Harry Truman did win friends in Washington. He worked hard at learning how the business of the government was accomplished. He attended committee meetings. He studied dry reports. In addition, he was always

47

willing to go out of his way to do a favor for someone else. By the end of his first term, he was one of the most well-liked men in the Senate. Many of his fellow senators felt truly sorry that he would soon be leaving them.

For it seemed out of the question that he could win a second term. At last, Tom Pendergast had been caught stealing money, and his political machine suddenly fell apart. In the confusion, half a dozen ambitious men were fighting for the Senate nomination out in Missouri. Several were rich, or could count on financial help from rich friends, and Harry Truman had no such backing. How could he possibly pay for an expensive campaign?

Even he appeared ready to give up. He told his wife she could start packing, but Bess Truman knew him better than he knew himself. Her husband was no quitter—and he proved it during the summer of 1940.

Once he made up his mind to run again, he never stopped working. He went back to Missouri and traveled day and night from town to town. He would not even admit that he might lose this race. What if he did lack rich friends? He was better off without any, he said briskly.

For he had already had his fill of being called somebody else's puppet. By accepting financial help from wealthy businessmen, he could be accused of merely changing masters. But now no one could doubt that he was running on his own.

Still he did need money. He had to hire meeting halls and get posters printed. To reach the largest possible number of people, he had to reserve time on radio stations. Who would pay these costs?

The people of Missouri!

Harry Truman said they would, and political experts shook their heads. "Not a chance," they murmured wisely.

Then mail from every part of the state began arriving at Truman's campaign headquarters in Kansas City. Volunteer workers counted out the stacks of crumpled dollar bills sent by ordinary citizens. As autumn approached and Truman kept up his appeals, the sacks of letters grew heavier and heavier.

It seemed that a good many people really did want to help Harry Truman. But the political experts would not change their minds. "He can't win," they still told each other.

Truman himself thought differently. He was

Smiling Senator Truman, with his wife, is holding some
telegrams congratulating him on his victory. *Harry S. Truman Library*

sure that if he talked his own brand of common sense at every crossroads, the people would vote for him. So he hammered away on two basic issues.

As far as the nation's problems at home were concerned, he said President Roosevelt's New Deal provided the best hope for improving the lot of the average person. He promised to continue supporting Roosevelt wholeheartedly.

However, foreign problems were becoming increasingly urgent. Another great war had started in Europe just a year earlier, in 1939. Truman could not forget how unprepared the United States had been back in 1917 when it was drawn into the First World War. While he prayed that American involvement could be avoided this time, he strongly favored taking steps to prepare for the worst. So he pledged that he would do all he could toward strengthening the country's defenses if the voters sent him back to Washington.

They did. With no help at all from rich friends or from the likes of Tom Pendergast, Harry Truman won a second term in the United States Senate.

8

...and Fact Man

When Truman returned to the Senate a few days after his reelection, everybody there stood up and cheered. Then the other senators crowded around him to shake his hand or to pound him on the back.

A reporter watching this unusual scene scribbled a note and passed it to another writer. It said: "They're acting like a bunch of schoolboys greeting a popular kid who's just got over the measles."

Senator Truman would have understood exactly what the reporter meant. By getting elected purely on his own, he had cured himself of "Pendergast-itis." Now he could speak up about government

Senator Truman playing a duet with his daughter, Mary Margaret, 1940. *Harry S. Truman Library*

business without being dismissed as only a Pendergast puppet.

In these last months of 1940, Senator Truman had a lot he wanted to say. For several years, he had become more and more disturbed by events in Europe. His long study of history made him regard Adolf Hitler as a terrible threat to the United States.

Hitler's rise to power in Germany had alarmed Truman so deeply because the Nazi leader gave every sign of being bent on conquering the whole world. Even before the start of World War II, German troops had taken over Austria and Czechoslovakia. Then in 1939, German tanks attacked Poland. Finally England and France accepted the fact that Hitler could not be stopped except by force. But Truman felt little confidence in Europe's ability to fight Hitler without American help.

Already France had been taken over by the Nazis. Belgium and the Netherlands and Norway were all under German rule. German bombers were raiding London daily. It seemed only a matter of time until England fell—and then what could prevent Hitler from trying next to stifle freedom on the other side of the Atlantic Ocean?

President Roosevelt, of course, was aware of the need to protect American interests during this critical period. He had already begun trying to make his country stronger. At his request, Congress passed a law requiring America's men to serve in the nation's armed forces if they were selected for active duty. In addition, factories from New York to California were rushing to produce supplies for the overseas friends of freedom and for the defense of the United States.

It was this matter of producing war materials that particularly concerned Senator Truman. He did not doubt for an instant that the nation needed a bigger army and better weapons, because the situation in Europe was growing more menacing every month. But he suspected that not enough care was being taken to prevent dishonesty, and that large sums of money were being wasted.

Soon after being reelected, he took a trip around the country all by himself to see if his suspicions were justified. They were. Everywhere he went, he found evidence that some greedy businessmen were overcharging the government or selling it second-rate equipment.

When he returned to Washington, he stood up

in the Senate and said that something had to be done and done fast.

"It won't do any good digging up dead horses ten years from now," he warned. "The thing to do is dig this stuff up now and correct it."

So he asked the Senate to form a new committee which would have the duty of keeping a close eye on money spent for defense. Because Senator Truman's words carried a new weight, he won approval for this plan and was also chosen as the chairman of the new group.

Its official name was the Senate Defense Investigating Committee, but everybody called it the Truman Committee. Because Senator Truman didn't think he could find out all he aimed to find out by staying in Washington, he and the other committee members made one trip after another all around the country. They inspected shipyards and factories and military training camps, always seeking signs of inefficiency or dishonesty.

"I'm tired as a dog and having the time of my life," Senator Truman wrote to his wife.

When the United States entered the war after the Japanese attacked Pearl Harbor, Truman worked even harder. Vast sums of money were being spent on the war effort, and he wanted to be sure this money was spent wisely. He made such a point of digging out the facts about war-spending that he became widely known as the Senate's "fact man."

Then people in other states besides Missouri began reading more and more about Senator Truman in their newspapers.

"There's no doubt that Senator Truman has saved the nation's taxpayers billions—yes billions—of dollars," one political expert wrote. Such comments had a startling effect.

President Franklin D. Roosevelt was a great reader of newspapers. He had never felt very friendly toward Senator Truman because of the Missouri senator's old tie with Tom Pendergast. But the president liked the way Senator Truman had been making his own job easier during recent years, and he also liked to read the kind words the newspapers were writing about this fellow Democrat. As a new election grew closer, President Roosevelt began planning a surprise.

By the summer of 1944, the United States and its Allies were beginning to feel certain of winning the terrible war they were fighting. Still President

Roosevelt believed he would be neglecting his duty to his country and to the whole free world if he retired now, and left the job of finishing the struggle in inexperienced hands. Even though he had already served longer as president than any other man in American history, he decided to run for a fourth term that fall.

He realized, though, that his decision would upset many people who thought just two terms were enough for any president. He also realized that Henry Wallace, his vice-president during his third term, had angered other people by speaking in favor of unpopular causes. To win the election of 1944, Franklin Roosevelt thought he needed a popular man to run with him for vice-president—and he picked Harry Truman.

Truman was staggered when he was told about this by the chairman of the Democratic party, who showed him a note in the President's handwriting saying: "Bob, it's Truman. FDR."

But Senator Truman had been in politics long enough to know what was expected of him. Although he was happy to be a senator and had never thought seriously of aiming any higher, he began making speeches all over the country while Presi-

Vice-Presidential candidate Truman conversing with President Roosevelt shortly before the 1944 election. New York Herald Tribune, *courtesy of Harry S. Truman Library*

dent Roosevelt stayed in Washington directing the war effort.

So many voters approved of this Democratic team that on January 20, 1945, Harry Truman stood on the steps of the Capitol and took the oath that made him the vice-president of the United States. Then, as soon as he could slip away, he found a telephone and called his mother in Missouri.

"Now you behave yourself, Harry," she said.

9

"Please Come Right Over!"

Three months later, Vice-President Truman finished presiding over a meeting of the Senate and then stopped in to see Speaker Rayburn of the House of Representatives.

Sam Rayburn was one of his oldest friends in Washington, and now that these two had so much to say about how congressional business was conducted, they had fallen into the habit of getting together late every afternoon. On this April afternoon, Speaker Rayburn wore a questioning look when Truman arrived.

"The White House just called," Rayburn said.

"They've been trying to get in touch with you, Harry. I wonder what's up."

Truman wondered, too. During his three months as vice-president, he had seen President Roosevelt only a few times. Roosevelt was so busy with the war that he rarely could spare half an hour for other matters. He had returned from a recent conference, and worn out by the strain of bearing such a heavy burden, he was supposed to be resting in Georgia now. Then why had his secretary just telephoned?

After quickly dialing the White House, Truman was connected with a private line.

"Please come right over!" President Roosevelt's secretary said tensely.

While he hurried to his car and drove down Pennsylvania Avenue, Truman decided that the president must have returned to Washington unexpectedly. Probably he wanted to give his vice-president some background information about a new development in the war. But when Truman entered the White House, he was taken immediately to Mrs. Roosevelt's sitting room.

Mrs. Roosevelt stepped forward as he entered. "Harry," she said quietly, "the president is dead."

Tears filled his eyes, and Truman could not bring himself to speak. Like millions of other people all over the world, he had loved Franklin Roosevelt. "Is there anything I can do for you?" he asked.

He never forgot Mrs. Roosevelt's reply. "Is there anything *we* can do for *you*?" she asked. "For you are the one in trouble now."

Ever since he had been asked to serve as vice-president, Truman had known this moment might come. Roosevelt had been under great pressure for a long time and might not be able to bear much more. But Harry Truman had not allowed himself to think about this. Now he suddenly felt as if the weight of the moon and stars and all the planets had fallen onto his own shoulders.

Yet he managed to do what had to be done. He telephoned his wife and asked her to come to the White House at once with Mary Margaret. He gave orders for the top officials in the government to be summoned. When they had gathered in the Cabinet Room, he stepped forward, raised his right hand, and in a firm voice he repeated the words that Chief Justice Stone read to him. At 7:09 P.M. on April 12, 1945, Harry Truman of Missouri became the president of the United States.

Outwardly, he seemed remarkably calm. He had to start making important decisions that very evening, and he made them without hesitation. The secretary of state, looking extremely worried, reminded him that plans were well underway for holding a meeting of delegates from many countries in San Francisco at the end of the month. A world organization that would have the great task of trying to ward off future wars was supposed to be founded there. President Roosevelt had taken a deep personal interest in setting up the new United Nations. Now how could the plans be carried out? "We'll go right ahead with the meeting," Truman told him.

But the new president gave a hint about how he was really feeling when he passed a group of reporters in a corridor. He stopped and said, "Boys, if you ever pray, pray for me now."

This remark was printed in newspapers all around the country, and it helped to make President Truman's first months in office even harder than they might otherwise have been. Many people mistook his modesty for a lack of self-confidence. They forgot that almost any man who followed Franklin Roosevelt into the White House was bound to seem weak because Roosevelt had been an extremely strong president.

But Truman had to rise above other disadvantages, too. No other vice-president in history had succeeded to the presidency while the country was facing such awesome problems. The greatest war ever fought was nearing its end, and the president of the United States had to make decisions affecting the future of all mankind. Nothing in the background of Harry Truman seemed to prepare him for such a terrible responsibility.

Although Truman had been a popular senator, he quickly discovered that this popularity did not carry over into the presidency. Hardly anybody thought that he was big enough for the job. Sarcastic comments about "the little man from Missouri" were heard everywhere.

In the inner councils of the government, though, some officials soon began wondering whether Harry Truman might not surprise the public. Without pretending to be wiser than he was, Truman listened carefully to the facts about every issue and then he swiftly decided what ought to be done.

He set the strategy that led to Germany's surrender in May. Two months later, he went to the

German city of Potsdam and met with two of the most commanding figures of the twentieth century. One was Winston Churchill, who had given England the heart to fight on toward victory. The other was Josef Stalin, the Soviet dictator who had joined the Allied side after Hitler attacked Russia. Now that victory over the Nazi forces had been won, both of these men were set on achieving their own special aims. But Harry Truman of Missouri took second place to nobody.

It was at Potsdam that Truman received a fateful message. Right after assuming the presidency, he had learned for the first time about a top-secret project. In strictly guarded laboratories, scientists were trying to unlock the mystery of atomic power. While Truman was conferring with Churchill and Stalin, an aide handed him a slip of paper informing him that these efforts had finally succeeded.

An atomic bomb had been exploded over an empty area of the New Mexico desert.

The most awesome weapon imaginable had been tested—and it worked.

Truman realized instantly that now he had to make one of the hardest decisions any man had ever made. In the Pacific, Japanese troops were still fighting fiercely. *Should the terrible new atomic bomb be used against Japan?*

No one else but the president of the United States could give the answer to this question.

Truman had never backed away from facing any difficult choice. On the other hand, he did not believe in jumping to conclusions without knowing all of the facts. So he gave Churchill and Stalin only a brief hint about the contents of the message he had just received from New Mexico.

As soon as he could, he consulted privately with his chief military and scientific advisors. He asked them how many American soldiers might be killed if the atomic bomb were not used and Japan had to be invaded from the sea before it surrendered. He was told the bomb might save a quarter of a million American lives.

All of his top military aides advised him to give the order for dropping one of the new bombs. Some scientists agreed, but others did not. They voiced the fear that the new weapon would horrify people in other lands because it would surely kill several hundred thousand Japanese men, women and children if it were exploded over a city of any size.

President Truman, with his top aides, announcing the end of World War II. *Harry S. Truman Library*

"I gave careful thought to what my advisors had counseled," Truman said later. The result was that he decided to issue a warning to Japan from the White House. In a solemn statement, he told the enemy nation to lay down its arms or a fearful new weapon would be used against it. He did this early in August of 1945.

Japan's rulers gave no sign of heeding his warning. So President Truman ordered the American Air Force to go ahead. On August 6, an atomic bomb was dropped on the Japanese city of Hiroshima, almost totally destroying it. Three days

later, a second bomb was dropped on Nagasaki.

Then the Japanese surrendered, and World War II was over!

When President Truman announced the great news, an excited crowd gathered outside the White House gates. Walking out onto the lawn with Mrs. Truman, the president grinned broadly. Then he threw up his hand and the fingers were spread in a triumphant V for Victory. At that moment, he was probably the most popular man in the United States.

10

"The Buck Stops Here"

Even before all the excitement about the end of the war was over, President Truman called together his closest advisers and told them, "Now we have to get busy on a new program."

He outlined a series of plans he had been thinking about during his early morning walks around the White House grounds. It seemed to him there were several different goals he should be aiming for.

In the first place, he wanted to see the change from war to peace go as smoothly as possible. Toward this end, he wanted the wartime government controls on prices to be continued until industry could get back to producing cars and refrigerators instead of tanks and guns. Otherwise, he was afraid the pent-up demand for household goods would force prices sky-high.

He also thought wages and profits should remain under control while the complicated shift to peace-time production was accomplished. Without such a "hold-the-line" policy, Truman predicted an un-happy period of hard times ahead.

In addition, Truman felt that a whole series of new measures ought to be taken to improve life for the average citizen. He reminded his aides that President Roosevelt had been trying to give the nation a New Deal when the war interrupted. With the return of peace, Truman said, it was time to pick up this unfinished business. So his own ob-jective would be to give the nation a "Fair Deal."

Under this heading, he asked his staff to draw up several specific plans to be presented to Congress. Among these were plans for a new national health system, for new civil rights protections to minori-ties, and for new federal aid to education. President Truman fervently hoped the law-makers would approve of these Fair Deal measures.

But when Truman's program was announced in

President Truman's plight as pictured by Roy Justus in the Minneapolis *Star*.

the newspapers, angry protests came from many business leaders. They were tired of following complicated directions telling them what they could and could not do. While the nation was at war, they had considered it their patriotic duty to go along with government rulings, but now they wanted the government to leave them alone.

Working people were just as tired of being told how much gasoline they could buy, or even how much money they could earn. Although Truman's Fair Deal aimed to help them—for instance, by providing a new system of free medical care—the great majority of people suddenly felt more interested in their own personal concerns than in any new government programs.

So Congress followed President Truman's advice on foreign affairs, but it did very little to put his Fair Deal into effect. Many newspapers even began poking fun at the president himself. They said he wasn't dignified enough to be taken seriously because he liked wearing splashy-colored shirts when he went on vacation, and because he lost his temper when music critics wrote unkind words about his daughter's singing. It was even reported that one evening in the White House dining room, the president of the United States had flipped a few watermelon seeds across the table at his wife, and she had fired right back at him, and a full-scale battle of watermelon seeds had gone on for several minutes while servants watching from the kitchen doorway stood doubled over with laughter.

As a result of stories like these, President Truman's popularity sank to a new low. Public opinion polls reported that only one-third of the voters thought he was doing a good job as chief executive. In every part of the country, people asked each other, "Have you heard the latest? To err is *Truman!*"

Instead of grumbling over the way he was being treated, President Truman managed to keep his own sense of humor. Realizing that much of the criticism he received would have been directed at any president who had to lead the nation through this difficult period, he put a sign on his desk that said, "The Buck Stops Here."

Even if he could have passed the buck to somebody else, Harry Truman would not have done it. He proved this when the presidential election of 1948 came in sight and political experts started guessing who would win. Not a single expert thought Truman stood a chance of being elected to a full term, but that didn't stop him. He decided to run anyway.

Despite all of the problems he had faced before, he felt that his record was pretty good. And it would have been even better, he was sure, if Congress had only cooperated with him.

Yet how could he convince the people of this?

President Truman figured out his own answer. He was positive that the people would vote for him if he could talk to enough of them, face to face. So he announced that he would soon be taking several trips across the country by train. His special train had an open platform attached to the last car. If any voters happened to turn up along the railroad track, he said in a sly tone of voice, then he would just ask the engineer to put on the brakes and he would step out onto that platform for a friendly visit with his fellow citizens.

The president left Washington in the middle of the summer and, except for a few brief intervals, he stayed on his train till election day. He rode thousands of miles, making speeches morning, noon and night.

At first, the crowds he attracted seemed to have gathered out of pure curiosity. They wanted to see what the president of the United States looked like in person. But from the days when he had run for office back in Missouri, Harry Truman knew how to capture people's attention with a few jokes and then a short, hard-hitting speech.

"My opponents say they have your interests at heart," he said time after time. "But don't you believe it for a minute. They elected the majority in Congress two years ago, and that Congress has done nothing. That lazy, do-nothing Congress is just a sample of what you're going to get if you hand the whole government to these so-called 'friends' of yours."

"Pour it on, Harry!" somebody in the crowd would holler.

The ordinary citizens of the country seemed to like Truman's spunky way of seeking votes. The crowds along his train route got larger and larger as election day grew closer. In the big cities he visited, tremendous crowds lined the streets to see him.

"Attaboy, Harry!" they shouted when he rode by.

A newspaper cartoonist pictures President Truman punching away at Congress during his campaign. The Detroit Free Press, *courtesy of New York Public Library Picture Collection*

When Governor Dewey of New York, his Republican opponent, came to town, there wasn't nearly as much happy excitement. Still the experts insisted that Truman could not win. They were wrong.

On November 2, 1948, Harry Truman won by a narrow margin. Then even his political enemies gave him credit for putting up a great fight. "You've got to give the little man credit," a leading Republican said. "There he was flat on his back. Everyone had counted him out but he came up fighting and won the battle. That's the kind of courage the American people admire."

11

The Winner!

For the next few months, Truman enjoyed reading the newspapers. Instead of making fun of him, they made fun of themselves and of all the "experts" who had been fooled by the election results. One paper in Chicago had been so sure Truman could not win that on election night it had printed a huge headline: DEWEY DEFEATS TRUMAN. A picture of Truman holding up a copy of this paper, and grinning his broadest grin, appeared on front pages everywhere.

His happiest day, though, was January 20, 1949. Before taking the oath of office for the full term he had earned as president, he had breakfast with

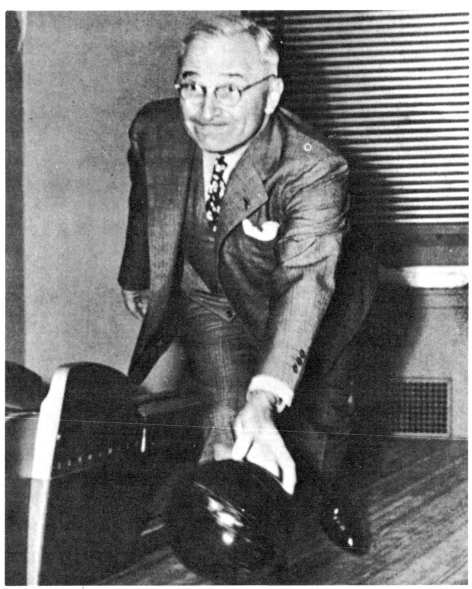

Taking time off from his official duties, President Truman relaxes at the new bowling alley built in the White House basement. *Harry S. Truman Library*

ninety-eight men who had been part of Battery D during the First World War. When these ex-soldiers arrived at the White House, they felt a little uncomfortable. Shaking hands with their former commander, they shyly called him "Mr. President."

"You'll call me Captain Harry just like you did thirty years ago," he told them.

After the excitement of being sworn in, and then a grand parade, President Truman again settled down to work on his Fair Deal. But foreign problems kept interfering with his efforts to pass new laws dealing with such matters as health care.

He acted firmly when the Russians blocked all the roads leading to West Berlin. By sending American planes loaded with supplies for the tense city, he showed the world that the United States would not abandon its friends in Europe. This was only one of the many steps President Truman took to try to keep the "cold war" with Communist Russia from erupting into a shooting war.

But on June 24, 1950, while he was vacationing in Independence, he received an urgent telephone call from his secretary of state.

"Mr. President," the secretary of state said, "I

have very serious news. The North Koreans have invaded South Korea."

Because the North Koreans were Russia's allies, President Truman feared that all of Asia might fall under Communist control unless the South Koreans were helped. He flew back to Washington immediately. The next day the United States urged the United Nations to force the North Koreans to retreat. The Russian delegates marched out of the UN meeting in angry protest. Then the United States offered to provide soldiers and supplies for a new United Nations army that would try to restore peace in Korea. Without any Russian delegates on hand to block this move, the American plan was adopted.

In every way except legally, the United States was at war again. Although several other countries sent small units of soldiers to Korea, the United States bore the main burden of contributing men and weapons for the United Nations forces there.

President Truman took full responsibility for America's involvement in Korea. When a reporter asked him if he could rest easy knowing that he had made this fateful decision, he gave an indirect answer.

"If you can't stand the heat," he said, "get out of the kitchen."

Nothing else that happened during Harry Truman's term of office generated as much heat as Korea did. His earlier decision to drop atomic bombs over Japan had deeply shocked many people in other countries, as some of his scientific advisors had warned him it would. But most Americans still seemed to feel he had been justified in using the terrible weapon, in order to cut short the most bloody war in all history. However, even among his strongest supporters, his Korean policy caused increasing head-shaking.

For after a series of fierce battles, when the advantage kept shifting from one side to the other, the conflict dragged on with neither side scoring any decisive victory. It appeared likely that the fighting might continue indefinitely. Truman's original decision to send American forces to Korea had been widely approved, because his policy of seeking to keep Communism from spreading was popular. Even so, his seeming willingness to let this small war go on month after month lost him many admirers.

It also provoked the hottest controversy of his

presidency. His "enemy" in this case was General Douglas A. MacArthur.

General MacArthur, one of America's most colorful heroes in World War II, had been commanding United States occupation forces in Japan when the Korean fighting broke out. Everybody expected him to be put in charge of the United Nations effort on the new front—and at first he surprised only the North Koreans by the vigor of his attacks. However, he was soon surprising his commander in chief as well.

The North Korean invaders had strong ties with China's Communists. President Truman—and his friends in the UN—wanted above all to avoid any move that would bring hordes of Chinese soldiers into active combat in Korea. General MacArthur had a different attitude.

He thought he ought to be allowed to discourage China from helping North Korea. He wanted to bomb Chinese supply bases, and he kept sending Truman private messages saying this had to be done if the UN was to win the struggle. Truman could not agree.

Then MacArthur went further. He began issuing public statements in which he criticized the President's policy. "There is no substitute for victory," MacArthur said.

These words started angry debate all over the country. Many people who were disgusted with the situation in Korea thought MacArthur was right, and that he should be permitted to take any step necessary to defeat the North Koreans decisively. But many other people held that no general had the right to disagree openly with the president of the United States. They said MacArthur was violating a basic principle of American democracy, which put the civilian president in a higher position than any military officer.

Harry Truman agreed with this viewpoint. In the first case of its kind in American history, he fired General MacArthur.

"Under the circumstances," Truman wrote to an old friend, "I could do nothing else and still be president of the United States. Civilian control of the military was at stake, and I couldn't let it stay at stake very long."

Still Truman expected that his decision would stir a great uproar—and it did. During the next few weeks some people kept saying that Harry Truman was the one who ought to be fired, and they urged their congressmen to consider removing him from office. Other MacArthur supporters tried to get General MacArthur to run for president.

After a few months, though, the excitement died down. President Truman calmly went on conducting the business of the government. In time even his most bitter critics admitted that MacArthur had gone too far and had deserved to be retired .

But even if Truman still felt capable of standing any amount of heat, he began looking forward to his own retirement. So he did not consider running again in 1952. He would be sixty-eight that year and was willing to let another man take over the hardest job in the world. Being a lifelong Democrat, he had a strong feeling that his successor ought to be a member of his own party. As far as he himself was concerned, he was perfectly willing to oblige Mrs. Truman by spending the rest of his days peacefully in Independence.

12

Back in Independence

When Mr. and Mrs. Truman stepped off the train in Kansas City on the day after Dwight D. Eisenhower became the president of the United States, there were people as far as the eye could see in every direction.

A band struck up "The Missouri Waltz," which had come to be the Truman theme song. People waved and cheered so enthusiastically that Mrs. Truman smiled at her husband and said, "If this is what you get for all those years of hard work, I guess it was worth it."

All along their route to Independence, people stood by the side of the road waving and cheering.

Other bands blared a catchy tune entitled, "I'm Just Wild About Harry!" Touched by the warmth of this welcome, former President Truman made a little speech when he arrived at his front porch.

"I'm home for good and I mean it," he said with a big grin.

He did. Although he had felt a twinge of regret as he turned over the presidency to General Eisenhower, who was a Republican, Truman found that it was a great relief to give up the cares of office. Now he could take his morning walk down the streets of Independence without a troop of Secret Service men marching at his heels. When old friends stopped by, he could spare the time to sit and trade happy memories with them.

Still he had too much energy for just relaxing. Every morning he drove to an office downtown, where he kept very busy. Because he thought it would help future historians if he provided his own account of the great events he had seen at firsthand, he wrote two thick books about his experiences. He also worked on plans for a new Truman Library in Independence, in which he would store all his official papers and souvenirs.

After it was completed, this handsome building

Mr. and Mrs. Truman on the front porch of their home in
Independence, Missouri. *Harry S. Truman Library*

attracted thousands of visitors every year. While writers and teachers sat quietly taking notes in the large reading room, family groups from all over the country strolled through the exhibit halls. Many of them were delighted to discover the solution to a small mystery during their inspection tour.

The mystery involved the former president's middle name. Most newspapers referred to him as Harry S. Truman, but what did the letter S stand for? Truman himself always wrote, "Harry S Truman," not "Harry S. Truman." Why did he leave out a period after his middle initial?

A chart displayed on a wall in the Independence library answered these questions. It showed that one of his grandfathers—his mother's father—had been named Solomon Young; and that several of his father's forbears had been Shipps. Then it explained that when Harry's parents named him, they had wanted to avoid insulting either side of the family. Instead of a full middle name, they had given him just the middle initial S, thus pleasing both sets of grandparents.

"So that's it!" visitors kept murmuring as they studied the chart. After they left the library, some of them drove slowly along the tree-lined streets of

Independence, hoping to catch a glimpse of Mr. Truman taking one of his brisk walks. If they were lucky enough to spot him, they received a cheery wave or sometimes a handshake.

During these first years of his retirement Truman tried to keep out of the limelight. He turned down many invitations to speak at meetings, but he did make some exceptions. Feeling that the country's future depended on its young people, he welcomed opportunities for talking with them. When they asked him how to get started in politics, this is what he told them:

"The best thing you can do is to study history, particularly the history of your country, your city, your state. Read all the history you possibly can, and also the life stories of the people who have played an important part in history.

"But for a person who wants to go into politics, the main thing is that he must be honest. Otherwise he won't make it."

As the years passed, the former president did take on one new duty—and he couldn't have been more pleased. He became the grandfather of four lively little boys, after his daughter married a newspaper editor. When his grandsons came visiting, he stayed home from his office to tell them stories and read to them.

From time to time, Mr. and Mrs. Truman went to New York or Washington for some special occasion. Then newspaper reporters gathered around him again, and he cheerfully gave them his views on the issues of the day. Their stories always made a point of how chipper he still looked, despite his advancing age.

In 1959, he celebrated his seventy-fifth birthday, and he was still going strong. Even though he had to cut down on his activities gradually, he still kept up with what was happening by reading the newspapers every day. And he had the great satisfaction of reading what many thoughtful writers said about his own presidency after the passage of time put those years in a new light.

While Harry Truman had been in the White House, most professors and careful students of history had dismissed him as just an ordinary man who had become president by a series of accidents. They thought he would probably share the fate of men like Millard Fillmore or Andrew Johnson, and be all but forgotten.

Yet by the 1970s these same experts had

changed their minds. Now they thought that Harry Truman had done a good job as president. His common sense and his courage were highly praised. It even seemed possible that he would go down in history as one of the nation's outstanding leaders.

As for Harry Truman himself, he had his own view about his place in history. He said, "I hope to be remembered as *the people's president.*"

Late in 1972, former President Truman fell ill. For three weeks he waged a valiant struggle for life, fighting with the same courage and determination that he had always shown.

However, on December 26, 1972, "the people's president" died in a hospital in Kansas City, Missouri, at the age of eighty-eight.

SUGGESTED FURTHER READING*

Gosfield, Frank and Bernhardt Hurwood, *Korea: Land of the 38th Parallel.* New York: Parents' Magazine Press, 1969.

Leckie, Robert, *The Story of World War II.* New York: Random House, 1964.

Moos, Malcolm, *Dwight D. Eisenhower.* New York: Random House, 1964.

Sullivan, Wilson, *Franklin Delano Roosevelt.* New York: American Heritage Publishing Co., 1970.

Van Rensselaer, Alexander, *The Picture History of America.* Garden City: Doubleday & Co., Inc., 1961.

*NOTE: The books listed are suggested for young readers who may be interested in finding out more about some of the great events and famous people President Truman was influenced by, but it should be noted that *Harry Truman* is largely based on family recollections and papers in the Harry S. Truman Library in Independence, Missouri. I would like to thank all those on the staff there who assisted me in gathering material for this book.

D. F.

Index

95